Aging in Strength

Navigating the Second Half of Life with Deep Purpose, Achievements, and Lasting Joy

By

Lisa B. Bennett

Disclaimer

The content within this book is provided solely for general informational purposes. Lisa B. Bennett, the author, has diligently worked to ensure the accuracy and comprehensiveness of the material. Nevertheless, the author disclaims any warranties, express or implied, regarding the completeness, accuracy, reliability, suitability, or availability of the information, products, services, or graphics contained in this book.

Any reliance on such information is at your own risk, and the author will not be held liable for any loss or damage, including indirect or consequential loss, arising from the use of this book. While efforts are made to maintain the book's smooth operation, the author is not responsible for temporary unavailability due to unforeseen technical issues.

Readers are advised to seek advice from relevant professionals tailored to their specific situations. The author encourages exercising discretion and judgment when applying information from this book to individual circumstances.

About the Author

A seasoned researcher focused on aging and well-being, the author's work delves into the intricate facets of personal development in the later stages of life. Combining academic expertise with a genuine concern for individuals' overall wellness, she explores the challenges and triumphs that come with aging, presenting a holistic perspective on the journey.

Her writings illuminate the complexities of aging, offering actionable insights for navigating life's transitions with grace and resilience. Advocating for a holistic approach to well-being, she empowers readers to embrace the second half of life with purpose.

The author's commitment to empowering individuals shines through her work, challenging traditional perceptions of age as a limitation. Her writings serve as a guide for readers seeking a deeper understanding of themselves, providing a roadmap for a fulfilling and purpose-driven life. With a profound dedication to celebrating the beauty of each chapter, the author invites readers on a transformative journey towards a life embraced with wisdom and resilience.

Table of contents

Introduction

Welcome to "*Aging in Strength: Navigating the Second Half of Life with Deep Purpose, Achievements, and Lasting Joy*" In this incredible journey, we're on a mission to rewrite the story of life's later years. As we turn the pages, we're figuring out how to balance success, happiness, and a sense of purpose in the second half of life. The idea of success takes on a whole new meaning as we navigate this uncharted territory, reflecting on our experiences, bouncing back from challenges, and discovering strengths we didn't know we had.

In these chapters of life, we face the reality that it's a mix of highs and lows. We're questioning the usual standards of success and happiness, opting for a more meaningful and fulfilling path. It's all about living with intention, finding your true calling, and creating a story that truly speaks to your soul.

"Aging in Strength" isn't just a book; it's an open invitation to embrace the ups and downs of the journey, navigate the twists and turns, and come out on the other side stronger, happier, and more purposeful. Ready to jump into this transformative adventure?

Setting the Stage for Embracing the Second Half of Life

Embarking on the exploration of life's latter stages necessitates a purposeful shift in perspective. Approaching this new chapter requires recognizing its potential for significant growth, self-discovery, and the pursuit of meaningful pursuits. The standards of youthful ambition give way to wisdom gained through experience, shaping success beyond professional milestones and intertwining with personal contentment and genuine happiness.

Moving forward demands a nuanced understanding of success, happiness, and purpose, challenging conventional norms. It's an opportunity to reevaluate, redefine, and align aspirations with authentic desires that resonate from within.

As we delve into the pages of "Aging in Strength," let's collectively lay the foundation for a journey that transcends societal expectations, unlocking the door to a fulfilling second half of life. This isn't merely a continuation; it's a renaissance—an opportunity to embrace complexities, relish the richness of experience, and uncover the true strength within as we navigate the uncharted waters of the years ahead.

Overview of the journey from professional success to personal fulfillment

"Aging in Strength" is a guiding companion on a transformative path, redirecting focus from conventional measures of professional success to a profound exploration of personal satisfaction. It navigates the shift from career peaks to life's second phase, offering insights and practical advice to approach this transition with purpose and resilience.

Early chapters prompt anticipation and preparation for the peak of one's career, fostering introspection about future aspirations. The "Second Curve" concept becomes a guiding principle, advocating adaptability and openness to new opportunities.

A central theme challenges the notion of success addiction, promoting a more sustainable and holistic approach to personal achievements. "Start Chipping Away" presents actionable steps, breaking down large goals into manageable tasks for continuous growth.

"Reflect on Your Mortality" encourages a reflective examination of mortality, urging alignment of life choices with a deeper understanding of existence's finite nature. The narrative then shifts to the empowering idea of turning weaknesses into sources of strength, fostering resilience and self-empowerment.

As the journey unfolds, readers learn to navigate challenges gracefully, viewing setbacks as stepping stones toward personal evolution. "Aging in Strength" is more than a guide; it's an invitation to reassess priorities, embrace change, and discover renewed purpose, ultimately leading to a life marked by enduring fulfillment.

Chapter 1

Your Career Descent Approaches Sooner Than Anticipated

You're invited to confront the impending transformation in your career. This insightful journey encourages you to identify the indications of transitioning from the pinnacle of your professional path to the next stage. Embracing this awareness enables you to make intentional decisions and navigate your career with foresight.

Investigating the Inherent Progression of one's Professional Journey

The organic progression of a professional life constitutes a diverse journey, marked by dynamic shifts and transformative phases. It doesn't follow a linear path but rather mirrors a continuous cycle involving growth, adaptation, and change.

Fundamentally, this evolution acknowledges that careers unfold in distinct stages, featuring peaks of achievement, stable plateaus, and transitions leading to fresh opportunities. Embracing this cyclical nature allows individuals to value the varied experiences contributing to the overall fabric of their professional story.

Adaptability is a central theme in this evolution, urging professionals to cultivate a mindset that welcomes change as an essential catalyst for personal and career development. This adaptability empowers individuals to navigate uncertainties, seize new opportunities, and remain resilient in the face of challenges.

Continuous learning forms a cornerstone of this evolution, encouraging professionals to engage in ongoing skill development, staying attuned to industry trends and emerging technologies. Commitment to learning fosters agility, ensuring individuals remain relevant and adept in an ever-evolving professional landscape.

Exploration and openness to new opportunities are integral aspects of this natural evolution, involving the embrace of change by seeking fresh challenges, whether within the current role or venturing into new professional domains. This spirit of exploration contributes to a sense of fulfillment and prevents stagnation.

Introspection plays a pivotal role in understanding the natural evolution of professional life. Regular reflection on personal goals, values, and aspirations helps individuals align their career paths with broader life objectives. This self-awareness becomes a guiding force, steering professionals toward decisions that resonate with their authentic selves.

Ultimately, the natural evolution of professional life invites individuals to celebrate change as a positive force. By recognizing the cyclical nature of their careers, professionals can approach transitions with resilience, wisdom, and a clear sense of purpose. This journey isn't about reaching a static destination but embracing the ongoing narrative of growth, adaptation, and fulfillment in the ever-changing landscape of the professional world.

The Significance of Acknowledging and Adjusting to Evolving Situations

Recognizing and adapting to changing circumstances is a crucial skill fundamental for success in both personal and professional realms. In life's ever-changing environment, unexpected shifts are inevitable, underscoring the significance of being capable of identifying and reacting to these changes as a valuable asset.

Acknowledgment is the foundation of successful adaptation. By recognizing changes in circumstances, individuals can confront reality, obtaining a clear understanding of the challenges or opportunities present. This awareness supports informed decision-making, averting denial or resistance that could impede progress.

Adaptation requires being flexible and resilient when confronted with change. Those who can adjust their strategies, perspectives, and actions in response to evolving circumstances are better prepared to navigate uncertainties successfully. This agility is especially important in the professional sphere, where industries, technologies, and market demands are continually changing.

Moreover, embracing change cultivates innovation, motivating individuals to delve into new ideas, adopt fresh approaches, and capitalize on emerging opportunities. This proactive mindset is a driving factor for both personal and organizational advancement, guaranteeing the ability to flourish in dynamic environments.

In both personal and professional relationships, being adaptable to changing situations improves collaboration and communication. It nurtures understanding and empathy as individuals acknowledge the changing needs and viewpoints of others, contributing to the creation of robust, interconnected communities.

Looking at personal growth, embracing change encourages continual learning. Adapting to new situations often involves gaining new skills, expanding knowledge, and stepping outside one's comfort zone. This dedication to ongoing development is essential for remaining pertinent and competitive in today's rapidly changing world.

Acknowledging and adjusting to shifting situations isn't merely a skill; it's a mindset vital for navigating life's intricacies. This approach empowers individuals to confront challenges with resilience, embrace opportunities with innovation, and cultivate meaningful connections through understanding. As an ongoing process, this recognition and adaptation form the basis for a dynamic and fulfilling

journey through life's constantly changing
landscape.

Chapter 2

The Second Curve

"The Second Curve" symbolizes a potent metaphor and strategic idea that transcends linear career paths and life trajectories. Originated by business strategist Charles Handy, the Second Curve proposes that individuals and organizations should foresee and navigate a new trajectory before the decline of the current one.

In the realm of personal growth, the Second Curve disrupts the idea of a singular, upward path in one's career or life. Instead, it motivates individuals to actively recognize and chase new opportunities, passions, or skills before the culmination of their current journey diminishes.

This idea acknowledges that the initial ascent and pinnacle of a career or life phase, represented by the first curve, will naturally level off or decline eventually. With this foresight, individuals are encouraged to investigate and welcome a second curve – a fresh path or set of goals that align with evolving personal or professional aspirations.

The Second Curve isn't about passively waiting for change; it's about being proactive and adaptable. It urges individuals to be ahead of the curve, promoting ongoing learning and a receptiveness to fresh opportunities. Through these actions, individuals can seamlessly move from one curve to the next, sidestepping stagnation and utilizing change for personal growth.

This idea holds particular relevance in today's swiftly changing and dynamic world. Industries undergo transformations, technologies progress, and personal priorities change. The Second Curve mindset empowers individuals to navigate these shifts with agility, guaranteeing a lasting sense of purpose and fulfillment.

The Concept of a Second Curve in Life

The idea of a second curve in life represents a strategic framework that disrupts the traditional path of a singular upward ascent. It prompts individuals to anticipate and actively seek a new trajectory before the natural decline or plateauing of the current one. The key lies in recognizing that life consists of evolving phases, where embracing change is not only a necessity but also an opportunity for growth.

Differing from the idea of a solitary, one-way journey, the second curve methodology encourages ongoing self-evaluation and adjustment. It involves understanding that the first curve, symbolizing initial accomplishments and peaks, will naturally level off. By foreseeing this, individuals can strategically steer toward a second curve, aligning with evolving aspirations and adapting to changing life circumstances.

This idea underscores the importance of looking ahead and taking a proactive approach. Instead of passively waiting for external factors to drive change, individuals actively guide their lives toward fresh opportunities, challenges, and areas of personal growth. It involves a purposeful effort to shape one's future rather than merely reacting to it.

The second curve is not a response to a crisis; it's a conscious decision to embrace the continual process of personal and professional development. It encourages thoughtful examination of personal goals, skills, and passions, cultivating a mindset that appreciates ongoing learning and adaptability.

In today's rapidly changing world, the second curve mindset holds particular relevance. Industries undergo transformations, societal norms change, and personal priorities shift. Embracing this concept involves being adaptable, maintaining curiosity, and using change as a catalyst for a more fulfilling and purposeful life.

Fundamentally, the idea of a second curve encourages individuals to be proactive architects of their life journeys. It advocates for a dynamic, purposeful approach, where each curve signifies a conscious step toward growth and resilience in response to life's unavoidable changes.

Examples of Individuals who have Successfully Navigated a Shift in Their Life's trajectory

Introducing Sarah, an experienced marketing executive who, after a decade of advancing in the corporate world, sensed a desire for a life with more purpose. Acknowledging the necessity for a second curve, she made a transition into the non-profit sector, utilizing her marketing expertise to raise awareness for social causes. Presently, she excels in a role that resonates with her values, illustrating how a strategic change can result in a more satisfying and meaningful career.

Meet John, an IT professional who experienced a sense of stagnation after spending years in the same technology role. Rather than settling for complacency, he initiated a journey of self-discovery. Identifying the growing need for sustainable solutions, he pursued training in renewable energy. Today, John stands as a prominent figure in the clean energy sector, demonstrating how a timely shift can result in a fulfilling and environmentally conscious career.

Introducing Alexandra, a accomplished lawyer who sensed an increasing urge to make a more direct contribution to her community. Overcoming challenges, she shifted from corporate law to become a legal advocate for underprivileged individuals. Through dedication to justice and unwavering perseverance, she successfully forged a second curve that not only resonates with her commitment to social equality but also showcases the transformative potential of personal reinvention.

Meet Mark, a former finance executive who discovered his genuine passion for culinary arts. Despite facing initial skepticism from peers and family, he decided to enroll in culinary school and launch a small restaurant. With dedication and innovative approaches, Mark's eatery garnered local acclaim, demonstrating how a courageous change in career path can result in both personal fulfillment and professional success.

Having spent years in a high-stress corporate setting, Emily made a choice to prioritize her well-being. She transitioned from a demanding managerial position to become a certified yoga instructor. Presently, she not only embraces a healthier lifestyle but also aids others in discovering balance and mindfulness. Emily's experience exemplifies how a shift towards personal fulfillment can pave the way for a more comprehensive and gratifying life journey.

Chapter 3

Overcome Your Success Dependency

This is a persuasive idea prompting individuals to reconsider and reshape their connection to success. Instead of persisting in an unyielding quest for external validation and accomplishments, this perspective advocates for a transition to a more balanced and sustainable definition of success.

Fundamentally, this concept questions the societal storyline that gauges success only through conventional indicators like wealth, status, or accolades. Instead, it encourages individuals to contemplate their inherent values, well-being, and overall life contentment. Through this approach, one can liberate themselves from the relentless cycle of continually pursuing external validations.

This shift in perspective entails recognizing that success is a diverse notion, involving personal development, meaningful connections, and a sense of purpose. It revolves around discovering satisfaction in the journey rather than solely focusing on reaching the destination.

"Overcome Your Success Dependency" Is an offer to rejoice in minor triumphs, value individual development, and prioritize well-being. It motivates individuals to establish achievable goals in harmony with their values, promoting a more wholesome and sustainable approach to personal and professional achievements.

Essentially, this idea supports a conscious and deliberate quest for success, urging individuals to establish their own criteria and resist societal pressure to adhere to external standards. By breaking free from the addiction to success, one can nurture a more resilient, balanced, and authentically satisfying life journey.

The Societal Pressure for Continuous Success

The pervasive influence of societal expectations for ongoing success frequently molds individuals' views, aspirations, and actions. In today's society, an implicit anticipation for perpetual accomplishments and upward progression exists, contributing to what can be termed a "success treadmill."

This pressure is driven by diverse elements, including cultural standards, media depictions, and economic frameworks. The dominant story frequently highlights outward indicators of success, such as career progress, material affluence, and social standing. Consequently, individuals might sense an obligation to engage in a continuous cycle of accomplishments to fulfill societal expectations and secure validation.

The surge of social media intensifies this pressure by providing a platform where selectively presented successes take center stage. The constant display of accomplishments on the internet can foster a feeling of comparison and an apprehension of not measuring up. This can result in individuals adopting the belief that success is an unending competition, allowing little space for relaxation or introspection.

The demand for perpetual success can likewise affect mental well-being, leading to stress, anxiety, and burnout. The apprehension of not meeting societal expectations may drive individuals to exceed reasonable limits, disregarding their well-being in the relentless pursuit of an elusive objective.

Furthermore, the societal focus on continual success may eclipse the importance of failure and the lessons gained from experiences. The apprehension of not meeting expectations might dissuade individuals from taking risks and being innovative, impeding both personal and collective development.

Tackling this societal pressure necessitates a cultural change towards a broader understanding of success, one that includes well-being, personal satisfaction, and meaningful connections. Promoting candid discussions about the complexities of success, embracing individual paths, and appreciating various forms of achievement can contribute to a more wholesome and balanced societal perspective. Ultimately, acknowledging the diverse aspects of success can help ease the unwarranted demand for perpetual success and cultivate a more supportive and compassionate societal ethos.

Revise Success According to Personal Standards and Discover Satisfaction Beyond Conventional Benchmarks

This philosophy empowers individuals to liberate themselves from traditional molds and chart courses that resonate with their distinctive aspirations and values.

This method prompts you to challenge societal expectations and understand that success doesn't adhere to a universal template. It invites you to investigate what genuinely brings significance and contentment at a personal level. By adopting this mindset, you can free yourself from external pressures and navigate a path that authentically aligns with your inner self.

The narrative advocates for a comprehensive comprehension of success, transcending material wealth or external affirmations. It encourages contemplating personal development, well-being, and the pursuit of passions as essential elements of a satisfying life. Success transforms into a dynamic, evolving journey rather than a fixed destination.

Discovering fulfillment beyond conventional metrics entails recognizing that happiness is a profoundly personal and subjective encounter. You're prompted to explore your distinct sources of joy and purpose, understanding that societal standards may not necessarily resonate with individual aspirations.

The philosophy underscores the significance of resilience when confronting challenges. Rethinking success involves embracing setbacks not as failures but as chances for growth and learning. It's an invitation to perceive the entirety of one's journey, including both triumphs and obstacles, as crucial to personal development.

In the end, this story acts as an empowering roadmap, encouraging you to take control of the narrative of your life. It asserts that success is most significant when it aligns with individual values and passions. By reshaping success according to your own terms, you set out on a path toward a more genuine, satisfying, and personally meaningful existence.

Chapter 4

Reflect on Your Mortality

This idea prompts you to view your own mortality not with fear but as a trigger for introspection. Contemplating the unavoidable end encourages individuals to reevaluate the importance of their daily decisions and long-term objectives. It acts as a reminder to live authentically, aligning actions with what genuinely matters in the broader context of life.

"Reflect on Your Mortality" Is a reflective idea that encourages individuals to ponder the limited duration of life and the transient nature of existence. It isn't a morbid activity but rather a philosophical inquiry aimed at cultivating a deeper comprehension of one's priorities, values, and the significance of the time we possess.

"Reflect on Your Mortality" Champions the significance of embracing the current moment and valuing relationships and experiences. It encourages individuals to liberate themselves from distractions that may divert from what is genuinely meaningful. Reflecting on mortality can act as a guide, directing individuals toward a life abundant in purpose and fulfillment.

Reflecting on mortality as a source of motivation

Reflecting on mortality as a motivational force is a potent mindset that urges individuals to use their awareness of their limited existence to drive themselves toward meaningful action and fulfillment.

Reflecting on mortality acts as a cue that time is a valuable and finite resource. Instead of instilling fear, this realization becomes a trigger for motivation, encouraging individuals to give priority to their aspirations, values, and relationships. Acknowledging the impermanence of life instills a sense of urgency and a dedication to maximize the present.

This mindset corresponds with the "**memento mori**" philosophy, encouraging individuals to grasp every moment and pursue goals with an elevated purpose. The understanding that life is transient becomes a motivating factor to venture beyond comfort zones, take measured risks, and engage in endeavors that resonate with one's profound desires.

Reflecting on mortality also brings about a clear understanding of priorities. It encourages individuals to let go of insignificant worries and concentrate on what holds genuine significance. Motivation arising from reflecting on mortality frequently leads to purposeful decision-making, nurturing a life that aligns more closely with personal values and aspirations. Furthermore, this mindset urges individuals to foster appreciation for the present and value the journey. Instead of fixating on the uncertainty of the future, those driven by the acknowledgment of mortality discover inspiration to craft a life that leaves a meaningful impact on both themselves and others.

Fundamentally, contemplating mortality as a motivational source changes the view of life's transience from a paralyzing idea to a guiding principle. It evolves into a compelling force for positive change, compelling individuals to live authentically, pursue their passions, and contribute meaningfully to the world around them.

Promoting a Conscious Approach to Life and Decision-making

Promoting a mindful approach to life and decision-making entails nurturing an elevated consciousness and purposeful presence in every moment. This mindset revolves around developing a profound connection with one's thoughts, emotions, and environment, facilitating more informed and intentional decision-making.

Embracing a mindful approach encourages individuals to accept the present moment without passing judgment. This involves recognizing thoughts and emotions without feeling overwhelmed by them. Cultivating this non-judgmental awareness enables individuals to make decisions based on a clear understanding of their values and priorities.

Making mindful decisions also means being completely immersed in the current task, devoid of distractions or preoccupations. This concentrated attention empowers individuals to make more thoughtful choices, whether in personal relationships, career paths, or daily activities. It's an opportunity to relish the depth of each experience and make decisions that resonate with one's authentic self.

Engaging in mindfulness prompts individuals to examine their thoughts and emotions with curiosity. This inquisitiveness unlocks the door to self-discovery, aiding individuals in comprehending their motivations, fears, and desires. With this self-awareness, decision-making evolves into a deliberate and empowering process.

Furthermore, a mindful approach underscores the significance of acknowledging the interconnectedness of actions and their repercussions. Individuals are prompted to contemplate the broader effects of their decisions on themselves, others, and the environment. This comprehensive outlook promotes conscientious and ethical decision-making. In the swift and frequently tumultuous world, a mindful approach acts as a stabilizing force. It enables individuals to navigate life's intricacies with grace and resilience, diminishing stress and improving overall well-being.

By promoting mindfulness, individuals can view decision-making as a deliberate and purposeful journey, contributing to a more fulfilling and purpose-driven life.

Chapter 5

Nurture Your Aspen Grove

A figurative idea urging individuals to foster their distinct strengths, values, and inner resilience amidst life's varying seasons. Drawing inspiration from the robust and interconnected root systems of aspen trees, this concept prompts individuals to develop a base of strength, adaptability, and authenticity.

Similar to an aspen grove, individuals are advised to cultivate profound roots – a robust foundation grounded in self-awareness and personal values. This foundation serves as a stabilizing force during life's unavoidable storms, offering a grounded anchor to withstand challenges and uncertainties.

The interlinked root structure of aspen trees signifies the significance of forging meaningful connections and supportive relationships. Nurturing an aspen grove in one's life entails cultivating a community of mutual support, where individuals derive strength from each other. This interconnectedness enhances resilience and promotes collective growth.

The metaphor is further reflected in gracefully embracing change, mirroring the way aspen leaves flutter and shift hues with the seasons. Nurturing your aspen grove is an invitation to adjust to life's natural cycles, recognizing that growth and transformation are intrinsic elements of the journey.

Moreover, the idea of the aspen grove underscores the beauty of individuality within a community. Each tree in an aspen grove possesses distinct qualities, contributing to the overall beauty and strength of the forest. Likewise, individuals are urged to embrace their unique characteristics and strengths, acknowledging that diversity enriches the resilience and depth of the collective experience. Fundamentally, "Nurture Your Aspen Grove" is an urging to deliberately foster inner strength, forge supportive connections, and embrace life's ever-shifting terrain. It's an empowering notion that prompts individuals not only to endure life's challenges but also to thrive, akin to the enduring beauty of an aspen grove.e.

Connecting Personal Growth with the Fortitude of an Aspen Grove

The robustness of an aspen grove offers a compelling analogy for the ever-evolving essence of personal growth. Establishing connections between these two reveals fundamental principles that enhance an individual's capacity to adjust, flourish, and withstand challenges.

1. Interconnected Support Systems: Aspen trees are recognized for their interlinked root systems, representing the strength derived from supportive relationships. Likewise, personal growth is frequently enriched through meaningful connections with others. Establishing a network of support nurtures resilience and offers a wellspring of strength during difficult times.

2. Deep Roots of Self-Awareness: Similar to the expansive root structure of an aspen grove, personal growth hinges on nurturing profound roots of self-awareness. Grasping one's values, strengths, and areas for improvement establishes a sturdy foundation for navigating life's intricacies.

3. Endurance Through Life's Storms: Aspens demonstrate resilience against challenging weather conditions, mirroring the concept that personal growth entails cultivating resilience to navigate life's adversities. The ability to withstand setbacks, glean lessons from challenges, and emerge stronger contributes to both individual well-being and the enduring nature of an aspen grove.

4. Adaptability to Change: Similar to the aspen grove gracefully adjusting to different seasons, personal growth entails embracing change with an open mind. The capacity to pivot, learn from experiences, and adapt to new circumstances is essential for both individual resilience and the enduring character of an aspen grove.

5. Flourishing Amidst Diversity: Aspen groves exemplify the beauty of diversity, where each tree adds to the overall magnificence of the landscape. In personal growth, acknowledging and appreciating individual differences enriches the collective experience. Embracing diversity in thoughts, experiences, and perspectives fuels both growth and resilience.

6. Continuous Renewal and Regeneration: Aspens are recognized for their capacity to regenerate and foster new growth. Similarly, personal growth constitutes an ongoing process of renewal. Nurturing a mindset of learning, evolving, and embracing new opportunities contributes to both personal flourishing and the sustained vitality characteristic of an aspen grove.

Comparing personal growth to the resilience of an aspen grove strengthens the notion that, akin to the interconnected trees in a flourishing forest, individuals can traverse life's dynamic terrain with strength, adaptability, and enduring grace.

The Significance of adaptability and cultivating a strong support system

The importance of adaptability and cultivating a strong support system cannot be overstated in navigating life's challenges and fostering personal well-being.

Adaptability

1. Embracing Life's Dynamics: Life inherently presents unforeseen challenges and opportunities. Adaptability empowers individuals to navigate these changes with resilience, turning uncertainties into avenues for personal growth.

2. Fostering Creative Solutions: Adaptability ignites innovative problem-solving. Individuals adept at navigating change are well-equipped to find creative solutions to challenges, enhancing the quality of decision-making.

3. Commitment to Lifelong Learning: Cultivating an adaptable mindset involves a dedication to continuous learning. Embracing new experiences and knowledge not only fosters personal development but also ensures staying relevant and agile in an ever-evolving world.

4. Navigating Global Dynamics: In our interconnected world, adaptability is paramount for understanding diverse cultures and global intricacies. The ability to integrate different perspectives enhances personal and professional effectiveness.

5. Alleviating Stress and Anxiety: The capacity to adapt mitigates the impact of stress and anxiety linked to uncertainty. Embracing change as a natural aspect of life enables individuals to approach challenges with openness and resilience.

6. Career Resilience: Rapid shifts in industries and job markets underscore the significance of adaptability in careers. Those embracing new skills and remaining open to evolving roles position themselves for long-term success.

7. Innovating in Ambiguous Environments: Ambiguity often accompanies change, and adaptability fosters innovation in uncertain landscapes. Those thriving amidst ambiguity are more likely to identify inventive solutions and seize emerging opportunities.

Cultivating a Strong Support System

1. Building Emotional Strength: A robust network of support acts as a crucial safety net during challenging moments. Emotional backing from friends, family, or a community aids in stress management, strengthens emotional resilience, and contributes to overall mental well-being.

2. Varied Perspectives: A diverse support system brings a range of perspectives to life's challenges. Multiple viewpoints contribute to a more comprehensive understanding of situations, facilitating well-rounded decision-making.

3. Commemorating Achievements: Support systems play a pivotal role not only during difficult times but also in celebrating successes. Sharing accomplishments with caring individuals creates a positive cycle, reinforcing a sense of achievement and connection.

4. Reciprocal Growth: A strong support system is reciprocal, fostering mutual development. Members within the network contribute to each other's progress, offering encouragement, constructive feedback, and motivation to pursue individual and collective goals.

5. Alleviating Isolation: During challenging periods, a support system diminishes feelings of isolation. Knowing that there are individuals who genuinely care and are ready to provide assistance offers comfort and a sense of security.

6. Professional Alliances: Beyond personal connections, a robust support system extends to professional networks. Establishing relationships within one's industry or field can provide valuable insights, mentorship, and career opportunities.

7. Involvement in Communities: Engaging with communities, whether local or online, expands the support system. Shared experiences within a community foster a sense of belonging and mutual support.

8. Mentorship and Counsel: Seeking mentorship establishes a structured support system for personal and professional growth.

Guidance from experienced individuals offers valuable insights and assistance in navigating challenges.

9. Diverse Insights in Decision-Making: A varied support system enriches decision-making by incorporating diverse perspectives. It ensures a thorough understanding of situations, leading to well-informed and nuanced choices.

10. Interconnected Success: Acknowledging interdependence within a support system reinforces the idea that individual success is often intertwined with the success of others. Collaborative efforts amplify the collective potential for growth and achievement.

Chapter 6

Start Chipping Away

In this chapter, we delve into the transformative power of the concept "Start Chipping Away." It acts as both an inspiring call and a strategic roadmap for individuals initiating their personal or professional journeys. This chapter delves into the profound influence of pursuing significant goals through gradual steps, highlighting the importance of tenacity, consistency, and the cumulative effect of small actions.

Effective Approaches for Instigating positive transformation and Progress

Embarking on a journey of positive change and progress is a deeply personal endeavor that requires practical strategies to navigate the twists and turns of life. Here are some down-to-earth approaches to kickstart meaningful transformations.

First things first, set clear and achievable goals. Break them down into bite-sized steps; it's like creating a roadmap for your own adventure. Develop a structured plan, a kind of game plan that guides your actions and keeps you on course.

Now, habits. Cultivate positive ones. Think of them as the building blocks of change. Consistency is key; those small, regular actions add up over time, paving the way for significant progress.

Prioritize and focus. It's like juggling—you've got to keep your eye on the important balls in the air. Avoid distractions that might throw off your rhythm. And speaking of rhythm, celebrate incremental progress. Small victories matter, and they fuel the momentum you need for the long haul.

Feedback is your friend. Be open to it. Learn from experiences, both good and bad. It's like having a compass that points you in the right direction.

Surround yourself with a support crew—people who've got your back. Their encouragement and insights can make the journey less lonely and more fulfilling.

Stay adaptable and open-minded. Life's a journey, not a rigid plan. Be ready to adjust your sails as the winds of change blow.

Visualize success. Picture it vividly in your mind. It's like having a destination on your GPS. It keeps you moving forward, making your goals more tangible.

Hold yourself accountable. Whether it's through self-reflection or sharing your progress, accountability keeps you committed to your goals. And when setbacks happen (and they will), view them as opportunities to learn and grow. It's like stumbling on a rocky path—you find your footing and keep going. Celebrate the milestones. Every step forward is a victory. It's like marking checkpoints along the way, reminding yourself that you're on the right track.

Breaking down large goals into Achievable Tasks for Consistent improvement

Imagine facing this enormous goal, like taking on the challenge of climbing a mountain. It's exhilarating, but the sheer size can be overwhelming. Now, picture breaking down that colossal goal into smaller, more manageable steps – almost like turning it into a series of achievable hills rather than an intimidating peak.

Why does this matter? Well, breaking down your big goal into these bite-sized steps brings clarity, like transforming a complicated puzzle into pieces you can handle. Each piece represents a task you can grasp, address, and eventually piece together to create the complete picture.

Remember how climbing that mountain seemed a bit daunting? Breaking it down turns it into a series of scenic hikes, removing the overwhelm and letting you focus on each step without feeling like the summit is out of reach.

Prioritization becomes a breeze when you break things down. Your list of steps allows you to decide which ones need your attention first – think of it as having a roadmap where you know your destination and the best route to get there.

Consistency is key, right? Breaking down goals encourages small, consistent actions, much like establishing a daily routine. It's not about sprinting but establishing a pace that lets you steadily move forward.

And those little victories along the way? They're like treasures found during your journey. Each smaller step is a win, and celebrating these milestones boosts your confidence, making you believe in the progress you're making.

Flexibility is crucial. Life throws curveballs, and breaking down your goals allows you to adapt. If something unexpected happens, you can adjust your approach without feeling like you're losing control.

Building momentum is magical. Successfully completing those smaller tasks creates a sense of achievement, much like rolling a snowball downhill – it starts small but gets bigger and more powerful as it keeps going.

Learning is part of the process. Breaking down goals gives you the chance to reflect on what's working and what can be improved – it's like going on a journey of self-discovery. You learn about your strengths, your challenges, and how you can grow along the way.

This approach also aligns with having a growth mindset. Challenges aren't roadblocks; they're opportunities to learn and improve. It's like looking at setbacks as detours rather than dead ends.

Lastly, breaking down your goals makes progress accessible. Instead of feeling like you're facing an insurmountable task, you're dealing with manageable steps – turning that mountain into a series of hills you can climb, one step at a time.

So, imagine that big goal of yours. Now, envision it as a series of smaller steps – each one taking you closer to the summit. It's not about conquering a mountain; it's about enjoying a series of scenic hikes, each step bringing you a bit closer to your breathtaking view at the top.

Chapter 7

Turn your Weaknesses into Strengths

Embrace a transformative journey with "Turn Your Weakness into Strength." This concept serves as both a guide and a mantra, encouraging you to view your vulnerabilities not as obstacles but as stepping stones. It challenges you to navigate through your challenges, fostering growth and empowerment. Think of it as transforming hurdles into stepping stones on your path of self-discovery and personal development.

Welcome vulnerabilities as Chances for personal Growth

Imagine this part as a deep dive into our shared humanity – an expedition that encourages us to view our vulnerabilities not as shortcomings but as extraordinary opportunities for personal growth.

It all begins with embracing imperfections. It's like saying, "Hey, I'm not flawless, and that's absolutely fine." We're letting go of the façade of having it all figured out and allowing ourselves to be a little messy, a little more human.

And what accompanies that acceptance? Self-compassion. It's akin to treating yourself with kindness when things get challenging. Instead of being your own critic, it's about becoming your own ally, especially in those vulnerable moments.

Then comes a remarkable shift in mindset – the growth mindset. Rather than perceiving vulnerabilities as fixed flaws, it's about seeing them as fertile ground for growth. It's believing in your capacity to change and improve, which is incredibly empowering.

Challenges become companions on this journey. Every stumble transforms into a lesson, an opportunity to enhance yourself. It's turning setbacks into setups for a comeback and gaining valuable insights along the way.

You become resilient. Vulnerabilities aren't indicators of weakness; they're opportunities to build resilience. It's like cultivating an inner strength that helps you rebound from whatever life throws at you, emerging even stronger.

And let's not overlook self-awareness. It's akin to delving deeper into self-discovery – understanding your triggers, fears, and areas where your strengths shine. This self-awareness becomes the roadmap for your personal growth expedition.

You don't have to navigate this alone. Embracing vulnerabilities is also about seeking support and connecting with others. It's finding strength in shared experiences and realizing you're not solitary on this journey.

Taking risks becomes an integral part of the adventure. Growth unfolds when you step out of your comfort zone, try new things, and embrace the uncertainty that accompanies personal and professional exploration.

Authenticity becomes your superpower. It's about being genuine, revealing the real you, vulnerabilities and all. And guess what? Authenticity fosters genuine connections and creates a space where growth can truly flourish.

Fear? It transforms into courage. Embracing vulnerabilities means confronting fears, acknowledging them, and using that energy to propel yourself forward. It's like turning fear into a potent force that propels you toward growth.

And you celebrate – every small victory. Every step you take toward growth, no matter how minuscule, is a triumph. These celebrations become the fuel that propels you forward, reinforcing your commitment to this beautiful journey of becoming the best version of yourself.

So, envision flipping the script on vulnerabilities. Instead of avoiding them, you're diving in, recognizing them as opportunities for growth. It's a bit like embracing your humanness and realizing that, within that vulnerability, you discover strength, resilience, and a path to becoming a better, more authentic you.

Leveraging life experiences for personal and professional growth

Imagine your life as a treasure trove of experiences, each holding a valuable nugget of wisdom capable of shaping both your personal and professional growth. Let's delve into how your unique journey serves as a potent guide for evolving into the best version of yourself:

1. Learning from Life's Challenges: Challenges are not roadblocks but rather stern professors in the school of life. View tough times as lessons. What did you learn? How did you navigate them? These challenges hold the keys to your resilience and growth.

2. Identifying Patterns in Your Narrative: Your life unfolds in patterns, akin to recurring themes in a compelling book. Recognizing these patterns helps you understand your strengths, preferences, and areas that might need a bit of attention. It's like deciphering your unique life language.

3. Reflecting on Highs and Lows: Take a leisurely stroll down memory lane. Triumphs and challenges alike, each moment has a story to share. Reflecting on these experiences provides a roadmap for making informed decisions in the future.

4. Transforming Adversity into Triumph: Setbacks aren't defeats; they're setups for remarkable comebacks. Your experiences likely include stories of turning adversity into triumph. These stories serve as your personal pep talks, reminding you of your inherent resilience.

5. Understanding Yourself and Others:

Relationships are the heartbeat of life. Your experiences shape your emotional intelligence, aiding in understanding both your emotions and those of others. This emotional insight becomes a potent tool in personal and professional relationships.

6. Navigating Life's Unexpected Turns: Life seldom follows a straight line. Your ability to adapt to unexpected twists is a superpower. Moments where you had to pivot become valuable skills for navigating the unpredictable turns of life.

7. Bouncing Back with Resilience: Resilience isn't taught; it's earned through life's ups and downs. Your experiences have toughened you up. Leverage this resilience to face challenges head-on, both in your personal life and your career.

8. Crafting Your Growth Story: Your journey is a narrative of growth. Each chapter, from educational pursuits to career shifts, contributes to who you are today. Acknowledge and celebrate this narrative of continuous development.

9. Pursuing Your Passions: Your passions often emerge from life's experiences. Leverage these passions to find your purpose. Aligning your life and work with what genuinely excites you not only brings fulfillment but also propels you toward meaningful growth.

10. Learning from Diverse Perspectives: Life exposes you to diverse viewpoints. Whether through travel, relationships, or work, these varied perspectives enrich your understanding. It's like having a toolkit of diverse approaches to problem-solving and decision-making.

11. Making Informed Decisions: Life experiences act as a compass for decision-making. Whether it's a career move or a personal choice, draw from the lessons embedded in your journey. It's like having a trusted guide steering you in the right direction.

12. Building Connections and Networks: Life experiences connect you with people. These connections can be your greatest assets for professional growth. Leveraging relationships cultivated over time opens doors to opportunities and collaborations.

Each experience, be it joyous or challenging, serves as a tool shaping your journey, aiding you in becoming not just older but wiser and more resilient. Your life is the best teacher you've ever had – now it's time to wholeheartedly embrace the lessons.

Chapter 8

Cast Into the Falling Tide

This is akin to immersing yourself in the spontaneous choreography of existence. It's about relinquishing the desire to control everything and letting the currents of change guide you. Envision it as plunging into the waves, relishing the uncertainty of where you'll end up.

That tight hold we often maintain on life? This concept encourages us to loosen it, welcoming the twists and turns instead of resisting. It's akin to saying, "Okay, life, let's see where you take me."

Flexibility is crucial. Life has its own cadence, and "Cast Into the Falling Tide" invites us to dance with it. Be flexible, bend when necessary, and ride the waves of change rather than standing rigidly against them.

Surrendering isn't about giving up; it's about finding strength in acceptance. It's recognizing the power in going with the flow, allowing life to unfold in its own way.

Ever pondered what lies beneath the surface of the falling tide? Similarly, embracing life's uncertainties can reveal new opportunities, hidden paths, and uncharted territories. It's an open invitation to explore the unknown with curiosity and an open heart.

Change is inherent to growth, much like the tide transforming the coastline. "Cast Into the Falling Tide" encourages us to embrace transformation, even when it arrives in waves of challenge.

Resilience is your anchor when the waters get stormy. It's about rebounding from setbacks, learning from the turbulence, and emerging with a newfound strength you might not have discovered otherwise.

Consider life's rhythms as a dance. Just as tides have their own beat, this concept nudges us to find harmony with the rhythms of life – the ups, the downs, and the steady moments in between.

Challenges aren't roadblocks; they're opportunities for growth. "Cast Into the Falling Tide" suggests that challenges are chances to learn, evolve, and navigate through the unpredictable twists and turns of life. Amidst it all, there's a call to be present. "Cast Into the Falling Tide" nudges us to live in the moment, recognizing that our power to shape our lives lies in the choices we make now.

Picture standing on the shore, feeling the breeze, and willingly throwing yourself into the falling tide of life. It's an adventure, a journey into the unknown, and a reminder that, like the ocean, life is vast, sometimes wild, but always filled with the potential for growth and discovery.

Navigating life's inevitable challenges

Life's challenges are a bit like sailing through uncharted waters, aren't they? Here's a down-to-earth take on how we can navigate those storms:

1. Making a Game Plan: Ever felt like you're navigating without a map? Creating a game plan, setting goals – that's like charting your course through life's twists and turns.

2. Flexibility is the Key: Just as a sailor adjusts their sails, we've got to be flexible. Life's winds change, and navigating challenges means being open to adapting your course.

3. Rolling with the Punches: Life loves throwing curveballs, and it's okay to admit that we can't dodge them all. Navigating challenges starts with a nod to the unpredictability of it all.

4. Lean on Your Crew: No one sails alone. Navigating challenges means reaching out to your crew – those friends, family, or mentors who keep you afloat when the seas get rough.

5. Lessons from Rough Waters: Rough patches aren't just obstacles; they're teachers. Navigating challenges involves learning from the tough times, picking up skills to sail through smoother waters next time.

6. Surviving the Storms: Storms will hit, guaranteed. Navigating life's challenges involves strapping in and weathering those storms, knowing that, like all storms, they will pass.

7. Cheers to Small Wins: Life's challenges often feel like a series of battles. Navigating them involves cheering for the small victories – acknowledging the progress, no matter how tiny.

8. Navigating Through the Fog: Sometimes, you can't see two feet in front of you. Navigating life's challenges means moving forward even when the path is unclear, trusting that the fog will lift.

9. Finding Calm in Chaos: Even in chaos, there's a quiet center. Navigating life's challenges is about finding that calm within yourself – a place of strength when everything else feels a bit crazy.

10. Enjoying the Scenic Route: It's not just about the destination. Navigating life's challenges is appreciating the journey – the highs, the lows, and everything in between.

11. Knowing When to Take a Breather: In the midst of chaos, dropping anchor is sometimes the wisest move. Navigating life involves recognizing when you need a pause, a moment to gather yourself before continuing the journey.

12. Challenges as Stepping Stones: Challenges aren't dead ends; they're steps forward. Navigating through them means seeing each challenge as a chance to grow, to become tougher, and to uncover strengths you didn't know you had.

Strategies for Resilience and Finding Meaning in Difficult Times

In challenging times, navigating the journey with resilience and a search for meaning is vital. A foundational step involves acknowledging and validating the array of emotions that arise during difficult moments; it's acceptable to feel a mix of emotions, and recognition is the initial step toward building resilience.

Building a supportive network acts like a safety net. Whether it comprises friends, family, or a community, having individuals to lean on fosters a sense of connection. Sharing thoughts and feelings with trusted people lightens the burden and serves as a reminder that facing difficulties doesn't have to be a solitary experience.

Practicing self-compassion is a potent tool during struggles. Treating oneself with kindness and understanding, recognizing that challenges are part of the shared human experience, offers the same care and empathy one would extend to a friend in tough times.

Discovering meaning in small moments serves as a source of strength. Even amid difficulties, there are often glimpses of joy, beauty, or connection. Paying attention to these moments, no matter how modest, contributes to a sense of purpose that can sustain individuals through challenges.

Engaging in purposeful activities aligned with personal values provides a sense of direction.

Whether in work, hobbies, or relationships, participating in meaningful pursuits contributes to resilience by offering a focus beyond immediate difficulties.

Cultivating a growth mindset involves viewing challenges as opportunities for personal development. Embracing the idea that difficult times can be transformative allows individuals to approach adversity with curiosity and openness.

Practicing mindfulness and presence grounds individuals in the present moment. Activities like meditation or being fully engaged in daily tasks can reduce anxiety and enhance resilience, serving as anchors during turbulent times.

Setting realistic goals is akin to breaking down larger challenges into manageable steps. It allows incremental progress, fostering a sense of accomplishment that strengthens resilience over time.

Learning from adversity involves reflecting on past challenges and extracting wisdom from those experiences. Understanding how past difficulties were navigated empowers individuals to face current challenges with a greater sense of capability.

Taking care of physical well-being significantly contributes to resilience. Ensuring adequate sleep, engaging in regular exercise, and maintaining a balanced diet support not only physical health but also positively impact mental well-being.

Expressing gratitude shifts the mindset from what's lacking to what's present. Cultivating a habit of acknowledging and appreciating the positive aspects of life fosters a positive outlook, contributing to resilience.

Conclusion

As we conclude this remarkable journey together, let's take a moment to ponder the profound insights we've uncovered along the way. It extends beyond redefining success or confronting challenges; it has been a deep exploration into the essence of our humanity.

We've maneuvered through the twists and turns of the latter part of life, challenging traditional ideas of success and discovering the power that arises from embracing our vulnerabilities. Whether facing the second curve, navigating the falling tide, or resisting societal pressures, we confronted them directly, recognizing resilience not merely as a shield but as a driving force propelling us onward.

So, what can we glean from these pages? It transcends overcoming challenges; it's about embracing the ascent, recognizing that the second half is not a descent but a climb to new summits of fulfillment and purpose.

As we conclude this chapter, let it serve as an invitation—a beckoning to approach the upcoming years not with trepidation but with a resilient spirit and a revitalized sense of purpose. Life's tapestry weaves together triumphs and trials, and in acknowledging this, we discover the wisdom to navigate with courage.

Allow the lessons inscribed in these pages to guide your path forward. Confront uncharted territories with bravery, face setbacks with grace, and relish successes with humility. May this journey be more than a tale read—it's a celebration of resilience and purpose, the true essence of a life well-lived. Here's to the chapters yet to unfold.

Leaving a Review

Dear Reader,

I trust this message reaches you in good health. I'm reaching out to express my sincere appreciation for opting to delve into this book. The journey has been remarkable, and I genuinely hope the book offered valuable insights.

As an author, your feedback holds significant importance for me. I would be grateful if you could spare a moment to share your thoughts by leaving a review at the place where you acquired the book.

Your review not only provides valuable insights for me but also aids other potential readers in discovering the book and determining its alignment with their needs and interests. Whether a brief comment or a more elaborate reflection, your candid feedback is highly valued.

Thank you once more for being a part of this journey. I eagerly anticipate hearing your thoughts and truly appreciate your time and consideration.

Warm regards,

Lisa B. Bennett